CW00959176

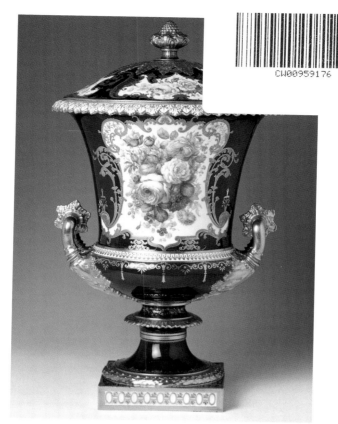

Royal Crown Derby. The 'Emperor' vase and cover. Sèvres-style decoration, large Campana shape. The reserves of roses and interior painting of morning glory and cornflowers are signed by Albert Gregory.

ROYAL CROWN DERBY

Margaret Sargeant

A Shire Book

Published in 2005 by Shire Publications Ltd, Cromwell House, Church Street, Princes Risborough, Buckinghamshire HP27 9AA, UK (Website: www.shirebooks.co.uk).

Copyright © 2000 by Margaret Sargeant.
Shire Album 376
First published 2000; reprinted 2005.
ISBN 0 7478 0443 5.
Margaret Sargeant is hereby identified as the author of this work in accordance with Section 77 of the Copyright, Designs and Patents Act 1988.

All rights reserved. No part of this publication may be reproduced or transmitted in any form or by any means, electronic or mechanical, including photocopy, recording, or any information storage and retrieval system, without permission in writing from the publishers.

British Library Cataloguing in Publication Data:
Sargeant, Margaret
Royal Crown Derby. – (The Shire book)
1. Derby porcelain – History
2. Porcelain industry – England – Derby – History
I. Title 738.2'7
ISBN 0 7478 0443 5

Cover photograph: *(Back row, from left to right)* King Street ewer, of similar form to 'Kedleston' shape, with acanthus moulding; the turquoise ground is painted with panels of roses and garden flowers by James Rouse; 1875. The Kedleston Vase (see page 9). One of a pair of the Barry ice pails (see page 13). The figure group 'Palemon and Lavinia' (more usually seen in biscuit) decorated by Samuel Keys; incised number N366; Robert Bloor, 1820. *(Front row, from left to right)* Royal Crown Derby 'Dwarf', painted by Mary Reynolds. Royal Crown Derby paperweight, 'Sleeping Kitten', modelled by Robert Tabbenor; introduced 1991. Royal Crown Derby chocolate cup, cover and stand; portrait cameo and flower swags painted by A. F. Wood; 1903. Superb pair of Royal Crown Derby musical trophy pedestal vases in Sèvres style; the reserves of musical instruments and flowers were designed and painted by Désiré Leroy; pattern number F508, shape number 1459; pink mark and royal warrant; 1906. Royal Crown Derby paperweight, 'Mallard'; modelled by John Ablitt; introduced 1997. Royal Crown Derby 'Dwarf', painted by Mary Reynolds. Royal Crown Derby vase and cover; pattern number 1128 'Old Imari', shape number 825; 1913; Myra Pedley Bequest. Royal Crown Derby paperweight, 'Pelican'; modelled by John Ablitt; introduced 1998. Royal Crown Derby paperweight, 'Cat'; modelled by Robert Jefferson; introduced 1988. *(Royal Crown Derby)*

ACKNOWLEDGEMENTS

I wish to thank the Royal Crown Derby Porcelain Company for their help and support during the writing of this book, and in particular: The Hon. Hugh Gibson, Managing Director, Royal Crown Derby; John Ablitt, designer, modeller, Royal Crown Derby; Elizabeth Parr, for her computing expertise on occasions when mine proved inadequate; John Twitchett FRSA, former curator of the Royal Crown Derby Museum, for permission to reproduce the factory marks from his books, which remain the standard reference works for students and collectors; Helen Lloyd, National Trust Adviser on Ceramics. Special thanks are due to my friend and colleague Joan Jones, Royal Doulton Curator, for her help and encouragement over the years, and without whose gentle persuasion this project would not have been undertaken.

I wish to thank Hubert King of W. W. Winters, Derby, and Gerald Wells of Northern Counties Photographers for supplying photographs. I am grateful to Anneke Bambery, Principal Curator, Derby City Museum and Art Gallery, for permission to reproduce the Gentian plate (page 12), and to Mr and Mrs Horsely, for permission to photograph the *Titanic* plate (page 34).

Printed in Great Britain by CIT Printing Services Ltd, Press Buildings, Merlins Bridge, Haverfordwest, Pembrokeshire SA61 1XF.

Contents

The Nottingham Road factory, 1750–1848 4

The King Street factory, 1848–1935 20

The Osmaston Road factory, 1877 to the present 24

Further reading 39

Places to visit 40

Principal dates

The Nottingham Road factory, 1750–1848
Andre Planche, 1748–56
William Duesbury I, 1756–86
William Duesbury II, 1786–96
Duesbury and Kean, 1796–1811
Robert Bloor, 1811–48

The King Street factory, 1848–1935

The Osmaston Road factory, 1877 to the present
The Derby Crown period, 1877–90
Royal Crown Derby, 1890 to the present

The Nottingham Road factory, 1750–1848

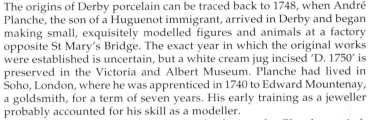

The origins of Derby porcelain can be traced back to 1748, when André Planche, the son of a Huguenot immigrant, arrived in Derby and began making small, exquisitely modelled figures and animals at a factory opposite St Mary's Bridge. The exact year in which the original works were established is uncertain, but a white cream jug incised 'D. 1750' is preserved in the Victoria and Albert Museum. Planche had lived in Soho, London, where he was apprenticed in 1740 to Edward Mountenay, a goldsmith, for a term of seven years. His early training as a jeweller probably accounted for his skill as a modeller.

Figure of a small charging bull modelled by André Planche. Date: 1750–5. Dry Edge. (Royal Crown Derby Museum)

Figures made during the Planche period, which lasted until 1756, are known as 'Dry Edge'. Derby, in common with the London factories of Chelsea and Bow, used a soft paste imitation porcelain and a thick and glassy glaze. As the figures were dipped in the glaze a narrow band at the base was left glaze-free to prevent fusing during firing, a distinctive Derby feature which greatly assists identification and dating.

Before 1760, unlike other factories, Derby made very little tableware and production consisted almost entirely of ornamental wares, vases and figures. The early body was unsuitable for tableware because it could not withstand boiling water but it was ideally

Pair of vases and covers. Reserve panels of Watteau-style figures within gilt and trellis borders on a gros bleu ground, applied flowers. Date: 1758–60. Patch marks. (Royal Crown Derby Museum)

Above left: *Fluted coffee pot, front painted with roses and tulips, verso painted with wild roses. Date: c.1760. Unattributed. (Royal Crown Derby Museum)*

Above right: *Large and forceful figure of 'Jupiter'. Measuring 18 inches (45 cm), this is one of the largest figures produced at Nottingham Road. Date: 1760. (Royal Crown Derby Museum)*

Below: *Blue and white butter tub and cover, the rectangular shape and canted corners painted in Chinese style in underglaze blue. Date: 1760. (Royal Crown Derby Museum)*

Right: *Figure group representing 'Autumn' from a set of the 'Seasons'. Date: 1761. Patch marks. (Royal Crown Derby Museum)*

Two from a set of three frill vases used for pot-pourri, decorated with applied flowers and painted by the artist known as the 'Moth and Bird' painter. Date: 1761. (Royal Crown Derby Museum)

suited to the art of figure modelling.

These early figures, such as the four 'Seasons', five 'Senses' and four 'Elements', were based largely on the European taste for popular themes. Figure groups in Chinoiserie style were also popular, as were the charming models of goats, sheep and wild boars. 'Dry Edge' figures are regarded by connoisseurs as the most dynamic examples of English figure modelling, with a freshness and vitality to rival even the finest Continental figures.

Derby's experiments to imitate the hard paste porcelain imported from China and Japan resulted in the discovery of soft paste, or *frit* porcelain, which was obtained by mixing ground glass and clay. Glass gave translucency and the characteristic 'ring', and clay gave plasticity and prevented the body losing shape during the firing, which took between twenty and thirty hours. Experiments to perfect the elusive white, translucent body continued and from 1765 soaprock became one of the main constituents of the Derby body, but it was calcined animal bone which proved to be the magic ingredient. Bone ash was added in increasing quantities until, by 1890, up to 50 per cent of the formula was made up of bone.

In 1756 Planche entered into an agreement with John Heath, a gentleman Derby banker, and William Duesbury, an enameller from Staffordshire. Duesbury had worked in London, where he owned a profitable business decorating to order china in 'the white' supplied by London dealers. His business had closed in 1753, largely because of competition from Chelsea and Bow, which, in common with other factories, were establishing their own decorating departments. Duesbury realised this trend could only escalate and was looking to move from decorating into manufacture

Left: *Pair of figures modelled as dancing Turks. Date: 1760. Patch marks. (Royal Crown Derby Museum)*

Below: *Large figure of the actor James Quinn in the role of Falstaff. Available in several sizes. Date: 1765. (Royal Crown Derby Museum)*

Under Duesbury's inspired leadership, the Nottingham Road factory prospered, achieving fame and international recognition. Production increased to include superbly decorated dinner, tea, dessert and coffee services, while the volume of figure production was surpassed only by the number produced at Bow. Many of the shapes, and much of the decoration, were strongly influenced by Meissen, and Duesbury claimed to have created at Derby a 'second Dresden'. Subjects included classical and allegorical themes, such as 'Europa and the Bull', 'Diana the Huntress' and 'Wisdom and Peace', as well as royalty, national heroes, saints and authors.

Blue and white china from this period is comparatively rare. The term is applied to china decorated with cobalt blue printed after the first firing of the clay but before the application of glaze. Richard Holdship, an expert in transfer printing, was engaged in 1764 to instruct the men in the technique of copper-plate printing, which was generally used on useful wares produced for the middle-class market, but Duesbury, who was interested in supplying mainly an aristocratic market, disliked the process and preferred

Above: *Large figure group 'Pensent-ils Raisin?' (sic). Based on a Le Bas engraving. Date: 1775. Chelsea Derby. (Royal Crown Derby Museum)*

Left: *A fine biscuit group of two lovers, 'La Bergère des Alpes', inspired by the Sèvres model by Étienne Falconet. Incised 126. Date: 1770. Chelsea Derby. (Royal Crown Derby Museum)*

Below: *One of a pair of ice pails made for Lord Cremorne. Delicate sprays of the period and armorial bearings. Date: 1780s.*

his men to paint the designs underglaze. Holdship left Derby in 1769, complaining that he was given little work.

The unglazed porcelain and biscuit figures, originally developed at Sèvres, were first made at Derby c.1770. The unsurpassed quality and beauty and the soft wax-like appearance of these early biscuit figures brought Derby international acclaim.

Keenly aware of competition, Duesbury purchased the Vauxhall, Kentish Town and Bow china works, all near London, and all of which he closed down. In 1769 he bought the famous Chelsea Works and brought craftsmen from Chelsea to Derby to improve the quality there and vastly increase production. It is a credit to Duesbury's managerial skills and business acumen that he was able to run both factories at the same time. He closed the Chelsea Works in 1784 and the majority of the remaining craftsmen transferred to Derby. Production during this period is referred to as 'Chelsea Derby' and is distinguished by 'patch marks' on the bases resembling thumb prints, formed by standing the pieces on three balls of clay during the firing.

In 1773 Duesbury opened a showroom in Bedford Street, London, which led to patronage from King George III, who authorised the use of the crown in the

Left: *The celebrated Kedleston Vase, believed to have been commissioned by Lord Scarsdale. The snake handles were modelled by J. J. Spangler, the rose swags painted by William Billingsley. The front panel was painted with a view of the south front of Kedleston Hall by Zachariah Boreman. On the reverse there is a panel depicting 'Virgins Awakening Cupid' by James Banford after Angelica Kauffman. Date: 1790. (Royal Crown Derby Museum)*

Below: *Very fine ring-handled teapot, pattern 40. Painted with Derbyshire views by 'Jockey' Hill and inscribed 'Breadsall, Derbyshire' and 'Near the Trent, Derbyshire'. Date: 1790–5. (Royal Crown Derby Museum)*

factory mark in 1775, and to visits from titled and important people.

Several months before his death in 1786, Duesbury had made his son, also William, a partner and, at the age of twenty-three, he became sole proprietor of the works. He had inherited his father's managerial skills and an even greater artistic appreciation. Building on the already formidable team of artists, gilders and modellers assembled by his father, he gathered together a workforce unparalleled in the history of English ceramics.

Duesbury II was a strict disciplinarian. In 1787 he imposed a fine of five shillings on any worker found in any department other than his own. Having assembled a gifted, highly trained workforce, and ever fearful of rival factories poaching his talented team (and ultimately his manufacturing secrets), he effected strict, legally enforceable contracts that virtually bound his employees to him for life.

Earlier models such as 'Elements' and 'Seasons' were revived and remodelled by J. J. Spangler, William Coffee and Gauron. All of the artists were extremely versatile, but those of note are George Robertson for his marine scenes, William Billingsley and William Pegg the Quaker for flowers, George Complin for still life and birds, Zachariah Boreman and 'Jockey' Hill for landscapes, and the Brewer brothers, John and Robert, for their landscapes, encampment scenes, animals and flowers.

When William Duesbury II died in 1796 at the untimely age of thirty-four, the factory had become the most important porcelain manufacturer in Britain, ranking high amongst the finest in Europe.

The celebrated Bemrose chocolate cup and stand. Painted with a view of 'Dovedale, Derbyshire' by Zachariah Boreman. Date: 1790.

In 1795 Duesbury had taken into partnership an Irish miniaturist named Michael Kean. Shortly after Duesbury's death Kean married his widow, Elizabeth, thus acquiring her interest in the business and her money. The marriage led to a family feud and a long and bitter legal battle. Disliked by the Duesbury family and unpopular with the workers, who feared his rages, Kean's tenure heralded the decline of the factory. Within a short time many of his finest craftsmen, including Spangler, Billingsley and Boreman, left. He was eventually forced to sell his interest and left Derby in 1811 to return to London.

Right: *Ring-handled teapot, sucrier. The yellow bands are overlaid with black scrolls and swags. A variation of the design was continued at King Street. Date: 1790s. (Royal Crown Derby Museum)*

Above: *Pair of lozenge-shaped botanical dishes painted by William Billingsley and inscribed 'Whoreled [sic] Correopsis' and 'Winged Padded Sophora'. Date: 1795. (Royal Crown Derby Museum)*

Right: *Ice pail and cover (cooler) from the 'Berlin' service. The coastal scene in pink camieu (a pinky brown) by John Brewer. The snake handles are modelled by J. J. Spangler. Date: 1809. (Royal Crown Derby Museum)*

Left: *(Front) Tea cup and saucer, pattern 269. Painted with panels of roses by William Billingsley. Date: c.1790. (Left) Pair of matching coffee cans and stands, unattributed. Date: 1795–1811. (Right) Timed studies of a running rose painted by John Sherwin. The artist was given a certain number of minutes to paint each study, adding progressively more detail as the time allowed was increased. Date: c.1800. (Royal Crown Derby Museum)*

Below: *Exceedingly rare yellow-ground honey pot and cover painted with a marine scene by George Robertson and inscribed 'A Calm'. Date: 1795. (Royal Crown Derby Museum)*

Left: *Teapot, cover and stand of unrecorded shape and pattern. The Meissen-style monochrome decoration is unattributed. Date: 1810. (Royal Crown Derby Museum)*

Below: *Important ice pail, cover and liner painted with views of, and inscribed, 'Denbighshire' and 'Shropshire' by George Robertson. Rich gilding in the form of vignettes of birds. Date: 1810. (Royal Crown Derby Museum)*

Below: *Teapot, cover and stand decorated with Imari pattern 'Grecian Rose', forerunner of Osmaston Road pattern 'Asian Rose'. Date: 1810. (Royal Crown Derby Museum)*

Left: *Bombe-shaped bough pot and cover with gold foliate feet and handles. The central reserve painted by 'Jockey' Hill. Inscribed 'Farm at Breadsall, Derbyshire'. Date: 1795. (Royal Crown Derby Museum)*

Right: *Large oval dish with gilt border and painted with 'Poppies' pattern number 197 by William Pegg the Quaker. Date: c.1796–1801. (Joan Shaw Collection)*

Below: *Teapot, cover and stand, signed 'Smith, enameller, Derby'. Blue and gold stripes and green swags. Date: Duesbury I period. (Royal Crown Derby Museum)*

Right: *Plate painted with a gentian by William Pegg the Quaker. (Derby City Museum and Art Gallery)*

(Left) One of a pair of the celebrated Barry ice pails, covers and liners. The running rose border is attributed to Thomas Martin Randall. Date: 1811. (Right) One of a pair of seaux from the Camden service. The running rose border is painted by William Billingsley. Date: 1790. (Royal Crown Derby Museum)

The Bloor period began in 1811 when Robert Bloor, a clerk to the Duesburys, leased and subsequently purchased the factory for £5000, to be paid in instalments commencing as soon as Bloor was able to raise the necessary capital. This he achieved by decorating large quantities of imperfect wares stockpiled during the time when only perfect wares were sold.

Bloor began his tenure at a disadvantage, lacking the managerial skills, artistic background and technical knowledge of the Duesburys. He had financial problems and was under constant pressure from creditors. The Napoleonic Wars had brought about a recession in what was a luxury trade. Bloor's battle to raise money is illustrated by an advertisement in the *Derby Mercury*, announcing a thirty-day sale, beginning on 23rd May 1814, in which a vast quantity of tableware, ornamental pieces, figures and five thousand items of whiteware were to be sold.

Above: *Figure of Edmund Kean in the role of Richard III. It seemed perfectly reasonable at the time that as the popularity of various actors waned the shrewd Derby manufactory appealed to popular demand by substituting the head of whichever actor was currently popular while retaining the body. The heads of David Garrick and John Philip Kemble are known to have been used. Date: 1815. (Royal Crown Derby Museum)*

Shell-shaped dessert dish painted with alternating panels of landscapes by William Corden and flowers by John Keys. Date: 1820–5. (Royal Crown Derby Museum)

Left: *Elongated Campana-shaped vase, richly gilt. The painting of a scene at Linsmore, Ireland, is attributed to Robert Brewer. Date: 1812–15. (Royal Crown Derby Museum)*

Below: *Small basket with gadroon edge. The border is in periwinkle blue, the landscape attributed to Edward Prince. Date: 1835–40. (Royal Crown Derby Museum)*

Left: *A pair of kidney-shaped dishes and a large basket from the Earl Ferrers service. Strongly attributed to John Hancock junior, who excelled in painting flowers and armorial bearings. Date: 1825–30. (Ronald William Raven Room)*

The Bloor years are often maligned because of the deterioration and discolouration of the body resulting from fine crazing which is often seen in the hardened glaze. However, Robert Bloor's contribution to the history of Derby china should not be undervalued. His tenure bridged an important period of change, when English manufacturers adopted the beautiful, translucent body known as bone china. The soft honey gilding of the eighteenth century was replaced by the much more hard-wearing mercury gilding, which burnished to a brilliant

Left: Lozenge-shaped dish painted with a view of Warwick Castle by Daniel Lucas. Date: 1825. (Royal Crown Derby Museum)

Below: Group of Imari decorated items: soup plate, butter dish, egg cup on fixed stand and jug. Date: 1820–5. (Royal Crown Derby Museum)

Above: Rare brooch painted with flowers by John Haslem. Date: 1847. (Royal Crown Derby Museum)

Right: Teapot with bun feet. Two oval landscapes painted by Robert Brewer and inscribed 'In Cumberland' and 'In Italy'. Date: 1820–5. (Royal Crown Derby Museum)

shine. Vase shapes became larger and more elaborate, while the flamboyant taste of Bloor's aristocratic clients was reflected in the new, heavy oil-based colour, lavish gilding and applied flowers.

Some very fine and richly decorated services were made at this time. They include a 250-piece service made for John, sixteenth Earl of Shrewsbury. Painted with fruit and insects by Thomas Steel, each piece has the armorial bearings of the Earls of Shrewsbury, and the magnificent

Superb pair of miniature portraits of Queen Victoria and Prince Albert. Painted and signed by John Haslem. Date: 1844. (Ronald William Raven Room)

ice pails formed as Warwick vases are a spectacular feature. Between 1820 and 1830 Earl Ferrers commissioned a gadroon-shaped service on which the floral reserves, central bouquets and coats of arms are attributed to John Hancock. The celebrated Barry family service, with its bands of running roses, is now attributed to Thomas Martin Randall. Queen Victoria is also known to have commissioned services. Other fine artists at work under Bloor include Moses Webster (florals), Richard Dodson (birds) and John Haslem (figure subjects and portraits). An

Watercolours from the 1813 sketchbook of William Pegg the Quaker. (Royal Crown Derby Museum)

16

Above: *A fine bombe-shaped bough pot and cover with richly applied flower decoration. Date: 1830. (Joan Shaw Collection)*

Above left: *(Top right) Plate of the 'Heber Percy' pattern, blue celeste border and very fine gilding. The centre painted with a Mundi rose. (Bottom) Very fine and rare plate painted with a moss rose and trailing ivy border. Both plates are dated c.1820 and painted by William Pegg the Quaker. (Left) Page from the 1813 Pegg sketchbook. (Royal Crown Derby Museum)*

Below left: *(Top) Soup plate from the Duke of Northumberland service painted by Edward Withers, c.1775. (Bottom) Gadroon-shaped plate, the central painting of a rose and apple attributed to Edwin Steele. Date: 1830. (Royal Crown Derby Museum)*

Below: *The unique Bloor Documentary Cup, painted by Robert Brewer with a view of the rear of the old Nottingham Road china works (1750–1848) in the early nineteenth century. This is the only known illustration of the factory in existence, apart from a lithograph taken from a sketch drawn from memory in 1870 by Moses Webster in his old age. The cup and its saucer have been kindly placed on extended loan to the Royal Crown Derby Museum by Hugh Gibson, managing director of Royal Crown Derby. (Royal Crown Derby Museum)*

Above: *Teapot with bun feet and monochrome decoration. Unattributed. Date: 1825–30.*

Left: *Large Campana-shaped vase painted in panoramic style with a profusion of flowers. Date: 1813–15. (Private collection)*

increasing demand for the lustrous and richly gilt 'Imari' patterns, introduced *c*.1770, forced Bloor to recruit experienced 'Japan' painters and gilders from the Staffordshire potteries. 'Imari' is the name of the Japanese port through which passed the richly decorated wares produced by the Arita potters; it became the collective name for the many variations of this stylised form of decoration.

Whilst these beautiful and expensive services brought prestige, they undoubtedly added to Bloor's financial worries. The difficulty of extracting money from his aristocratic patrons, who were notoriously slow in settling their accounts, eventually took its toll and by 1838 poor health forced Bloor to bring in his uncle, James Thomason, as manager. Under Thomason this once illustrious factory fell into steady decline. Bloor died in 1846 and the factory closed in 1848.

Shell-shaped dessert dish from a service made for the Earl Ferrers. The armorial bearing and flower painting are attributed to John Hancock junior. Robert Bloor, 1825-30.

Marks used at the Nottingham Road factory 1750–1848

Rebus for Richard Holdship. Found on transfer-printed wares; 1764–c.1769.

'Potters Stool'. John Twitchett, in his 'Derby Porcelain', states he has seen this mark on wares of inferior quality, possibly 'seconds' supplied to outside decorators.

Incised mark; 1765–85.

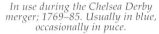

In use during the Chelsea Derby merger; 1769–85. Usually in blue, occasionally in puce.

In use at Chelsea; 1769–85. Usually in gold.

In use 1782–1825. After 1820 the previously neatly painted mark became increasingly carelessly drawn. Blue and puce were used until 1806, after which red became the standard colour.

Rare Duesbury and Kean mark; 1795.

Robert Bloor. Printed Gothic-style marks introduced to counteract the carelessly drawn marks; c.1820–48.

Pseudo-Sèvres mark used on Sèvres copies; 1830–48.

Marks used on Bloor figures. (Right) Pseudo-Meissen mark occasionally seen on late Bloor; c.1830.

The King Street factory, 1848–1935

Following the closure of the Nottingham Road factory, much of the equipment was sold to Samuel Boyle of Fenton, Staffordshire, but a small new factory was established a short distance away in King Street, Derby. Six of the workmen – Samuel Sharp, John Henson and Samuel Fearn (potters), James Hill and Sampson Hancock (painters) and their leader, William Locker (chief clerk) – joined forces to move production from Nottingham Road to King Street.

The new company styled itself 'Locker & Co, Late Bloor'. When Locker died in 1859 the partners took into the business a draper, George Stevenson, and the firm was renamed Stevenson Sharp & Co. This was later changed to Stevenson & Co, and in 1863 to Stevenson & Hancock. Initially the firm had used the old china works' mark of crown, crossed batons and 'D', but with this latest change the batons were changed to crossed swords with the addition of the initials 'S & H'. Stevenson died in 1866, leaving Hancock in control. Having the same initials, he continued to use the now famous 'S & H' as part of the factory mark, which remained unchanged until the merger with Royal Crown Derby in 1935.

Sampson Hancock died in 1895 and was succeeded by his grandson, James Robinson, who carried on the works until 1916. It was in that year that the first attempt to take over the company was made by its competitor, Royal Crown Derby, but the bid failed. The factory was sold instead to William Larcombe. In 1917 Larcombe took into partnership Howard Paget, who was in control until the 1935 merger.

The dating of earlier King Street pieces is extremely difficult, but with later pieces dating is helped by the following additions to the mark. Between 1916 and 1917 the letter 'L' overlaid with a 'W' was added to the factory mark, and between 1917 and 1934 a 'P' was added to the existing 'WL', and from 1934 a pair of crossed 'P's was added. Paget and his wife had pet names for each other, 'Peg' and 'Pug'; the crossed 'scissor' mark is said to be based on this. Occasionally the telegraphic address 'BCM/Pug' is found.

Sampson Hancock had firmly believed his new factory to be a continuation of the old china works rather than a new venture. From its inception King Street continued to use shapes and patterns in use before 1848, often retaining the original pattern names. Production included figures, dinner, dessert, coffee and tea services, and a wide range of beautifully decorated vases, pot-pourri bowls and pastille burners. Many were decorated with the richly coloured Imari patterns, which were

Large bottle vase and stopper. The painting of flowers and exotic birds is by Sampson Hancock's grandson, Harry Sampson Hancock. This very rare piece carries in addition to the usual mark a black Zeppelin and crescent moon and monogram because it was one of the items being fired during the Zeppelin raid on Derby in 1916. (Royal Crown Derby Museum)

Left: *King Street shield-shaped vase decorated with Imari pattern 'Old Crown Derby Witches'. This pattern was continued at Osmaston Road. Date: 1900. (Royal Crown Derby Museum)*

Right: *King Street dessert dish, the centre painted with a basket of flowers by H. S. Hancock. Date: 1920.*

The candlestick figure (left) holding a cage represents 'Matrimony'; it is one of a pair, the other (not shown) representing 'Liberty'. (Centre) King Street figure of 'Autumn'. (Right) Pair of Chelsea Derby figures, from a group known as 'Macaroni' figures. (Private collection)

21

King Street yellow-ground teapot painted with Chinese anemones by J. Wenker. Date: 1920. (Royal Crown Derby Museum)

more lavishly gilded than those of Nottingham Road. Favourite patterns were 'Derby', 'Rose', 'Garden' and 'Witches', all prefixed with 'Old Crown', a reminder, perhaps, of King Street's connection with Nottingham Road.

In contrast, much undecorated, glazed whiteware was produced: mirror frames, woven openwork baskets, bough pots and vases encrusted with flowers were modelled by Stephan (thought to be a descendant of the eighteenth-century painter Pierre Stephan) and Shufflebottom. Biscuit figures and small animals were produced but, although superbly modelled, the body could not be compared with the quality of the early Nottingham Road body: it was simply the standard, unglazed china body.

In addition to traditional figures such as 'Venus Awakening Cupid', 'Seasons', 'Elements' and 'Peacock', there was also a range of quaint and amusing figures, including 'African Sal', 'Billy Waters', 'Belper Joe', 'Greenwich Pensioner' and the various antics of 'Dr Syntax'. Combined candle snuffers and match holders in the form of popular personalities such as Elizabeth Fry were also produced.

King Street yellow-ground teapot painted with roses by William Mosley. Marks include the telegraphic address: BCM/Pug. Date: 1934–5.

Among the fine painters who worked at King Street were Sampson Hancock, who specialised in flowers, shells and birds; Frederick Chivers, fruit and flowers; W. Hargreave, birds; J. Ratcliffe, George Jessop, F. Schofield and A. Machin, naturalistic flowers and other subjects. Albert Haddock, one of the finest twentieth-century gilders, and James Rouse senior, who was the only artist to have worked at all three factories, were among the numerous craftsmen who transferred to Osmaston Road after the successful merger with Royal Crown Derby in 1935.

Marks used at the King Street factory 1848–1935

Locker, late Bloor; 1848–59.

Stevenson and Sharp; 1859–66.

Stevenson and Hancock; 1865–6.
Thereafter Sampson Hancock; 1866–1935

The following marks were sometimes added:

 William Larcombe; 1916.

 Larcombe and Paget; 1917–34.

 Paget; 1934.

'Peacock among Flowers'. Originally modelled by John Whitaker at Nottingham Road between 1829 and 1847. The original mould was among those acquired by William Locker and it was subsequently produced at King Street, making a pair. The models of both birds were brought to Osmaston Road when the King Street works were acquired in 1935 and in the late 1990s were still in production. (Royal Crown Derby Museum)

The Osmaston Road factory, 1877 to the present

THE DERBY CROWN PERIOD, 1877-1890

Plans to establish a modern china factory in Derby began in 1875 when Edward Phillips, a joint managing director of the Royal Worcester Porcelain Company, resigned following a confrontation with his co-managing director, Richard Binns, and entered into a partnership with William Litherland. Litherland came from a family of successful Liverpool glass and china retailers and was a major customer of Royal Worcester. They were joined towards the end of 1875 by John McInnes, a wealthy, highly respected Liverpool man who had a keen interest in china and a sound knowledge of chemistry.

Phillips believed that a factory should not be a 'dark Satanic mill', and his dream of establishing the most modern factory in Europe – a garden factory filled with natural light and having modern sanitation – came closer to realisation with the purchase, first, of 1^1/2 acres (0.6 hectare) of land on Osmaston Road adjacent to the Derby Workhouse

Derby Crown eggshell coffee cup and saucer. The salmon ground is decorated with raised paste gilding in the form of cornucopia, flowers and swags and beads. Date: 1888. (Royal Crown Derby Museum)

Derby Crown plate entitled 'Pity', painted by James Rouse senior. Date: 1880s. (Ronald William Raven Room)

and later, in 1876, of the workhouse itself, together with an extensive plot of land. After a year of setbacks and opposition from the local authority the new factory finally went into production in 1877, styling itself the Derby Crown Porcelain Company Limited.

Many innovative and interesting developments took place during the Derby Crown period. Perhaps the most important was the introduction of printed decoration on a scale so great that a special department was set up and an engraver permanently employed. Whilst the technique had been known since the earliest days, production had previously been for a strictly upper-class market. Now printing opened up a huge, hitherto untapped market, enabling an average family to purchase beautifully decorated tableware and ornaments at relatively low cost. At the same time, the introduction of an earthenware body further reduced the cost. Crown Earthenware is easily distinguishable as it was always marked with an incised crown. Production of earthenware ceased by 1910.

Copper-plate printing had two advantages. Firstly, once the plate had been engraved, beautiful and intricate patterns could be produced quickly, cheaply and easily, particularly where monochrome colours were used. Secondly, it could be used to produce borders as a decoration in their own right or outlines for gilders to follow. Previously, outlines for borders and centres had been sketched in by senior artists, a time-consuming and expensive process, but fine printed outlines enabled the details to be hand-painted by less experienced artists. An offshoot of printing was a process known as 'print and tint', whereby the majority of the design was printed, but small significant areas were left blank for enamelling by hand. Among the most popular designs were the blue and white 'Wilmot', 'Derby Lily', 'Derby Daisy', 'Peacock', 'Osborne' and 'Victoria', as well as the famous 'Mikado'.

Derby Crown. Group of Parian figures. (Left to right) 'Little Dorritt', 'The Love Letter' and 'Sally in Our Alley'. Date: unmarked. (Royal Crown Derby Museum)

Parian ware, so named because it closely resembled the creamy marble quarried on the Greek island of Paros, is reputed to have been invented by John Mountford, who had been apprenticed as a modeller at King Street, whilst he was working at Copeland, where he was experimenting to rediscover the eighteenth-century formula for Derby biscuit figures. Relatively inexpensive to produce because of its high glass content, washable and easy to work, Parian was eminently suitable for satisfying the demand for classical figures currently fuelled by the Victorian passion for statuary and sentimental figures such as 'Little Dorritt', 'The Love Letter' and 'Sally in Our Alley'. The modelling qualities of Parian also made it a perfect medium for brooches, delicate flower-filled baskets and intaglio plaques.

The Derby Crown years were a period of great experimental activity, when designers and modellers looked to the East for inspiration. The Number 1 Shape Book has many examples showing the strong Indian, Islamic and Persian influence which dominated production for more than twenty years. Magnificent vases of exotic shape, often of large size, were embellished with handles formed as elephant and tiger heads, entwined snakes and mongooses. Other examples had elaborately shaped, intricately pierced covers, bases and handles inspired by the domes,

latticed screens and carvings of Indian palaces and the Taj Mahal.

Above: *Derby tête-à-tête set decorated with Imari pattern 198. Date: 1886. (Royal Crown Derby Museum)*

Left: *Derby Crown moustache cup and saucer decorated with Imari pattern 383, later named 'King's' pattern. A pierced inset adjacent to the rim protected a gentleman's moustache from collecting tea leaves. Date: 1890. (Royal Crown Derby Museum)*

A factory duplicate of a plate from the celebrated Gladstone service. The painting of Pickering Tor is by Count Holtzendorff, the posy medallions by James Rouse senior. A number of extra plates and duplicates were painted by the same artists. Date: 1883. (Royal Crown Derby Museum)

Rich, jewel-coloured grounds of mazarine, Prussian and cobalt blue, ochre, coral, Siam and jade green were used, either singly or in harmonious combination. Ornamented with heavily raised, chased gilding, most brilliantly executed, the designs were inspired by the birds, flowers, insects and traditional motifs seen on priceless carpets and embroideries. Never before had the art of the craftsmen gilders been utilised to greater or more extravagant effect.

Raised and reraised gilding, so much a hallmark of the period, was achieved by using a paste made from glass frits, ground enamel colour and a small quantity of flux (to speed the process) bound together with turpentine. The paste was applied to the hand-drawn or smoke-printed design using a fine sable brush, after which it was fired through the enamel kiln. The process was then repeated until the desired effect was achieved and the whole design was then covered in pure gold. During the firing the oils added to the gold would burn off leaving a thin matt 'crust' on the surface. This was removed by hand burnishing, using fine white sand.

Yet another innovation at this time was the introduction of the eggshell body, a body so thin and translucent that the decoration can clearly be seen from the inside. The fact that so many of these exquisite pieces have survived unscathed is undoubtedly a tribute to the highly ornamental nature of the decoration, which has made them greatly prized by connoisseurs. Mainly used for coffee sets, each cup and saucer are miniature masterpieces executed by only the finest craftsmen. The decoration usually covers the entire surface, combining raised and flat gilding, gold studding and jewelling, often augmented with miniature portrait medallions.

Among the many distinguished services at this time, the celebrated Gladstone dessert service is arguably the finest. Commissioned by the Liberal Working Men of Derby to mark Prime Minister Gladstone's fifty years in politics and designed by Richard Lunn, each of the eighteen plates, four tall and four low comports was painted with a different Derbyshire view by Count Holtzendorff. The seventy-eight different miniature oval posy medallions adorning the borders were painted by James Rouse senior. Interspersed between the posies, the initials 'W.E.G.' worked in raised gold are set within jewelled oblong panels within

A very rare figure of a lady billiards player modelled by H. Warrington Hogg. An innovation for Derby, the figure is without a base, relying on the hem of the skirt and feet for balance. Date: 1880. (Royal Crown Derby Museum)

double borders of acid-etched gold.

The new factory attracted many fine painters, among them Count Holtzendorff, a Saxon nobleman specialising in landscapes, figure subjects and cherubs, and G. Landgraf, who painted portrait and figure subjects. Both were distinguished artists who fled to England in the aftermath of the Franco-Prussian War. James Rouse senior, who had worked at Nottingham Road and King Street, was over eighty when he was selected to paint the Gladstone service. John Porter Wale painted flowers, landscapes and cottage garden scenes using a delicate watercolour style in a palette of pastel pinks, lavenders, blues, greys and soft greens. He was also a fine watercolourist and later became head painter, designing many delicate patterns. George Darlington was responsible for much lovely flower painting, especially roses, and he was also a fine gilder.

Derby Crown. Front and back views of one of a pair of tall, elaborate vases. Richly gilt, 'jewelled' and intricately pierced, the vase is painted with classical figures by J. Platts. Date: 1888. (Royal Crown Derby Museum)

Royal Crown Derby. A very fine pair of wing-handled, ewer-shaped vases, superbly painted with flowers on an ivory ground by Désiré Leroy in what is known as his 'atmospheric style'. Date: 1891. (Royal Crown Derby Museum)

ROYAL CROWN DERBY FROM 1890

In 1887 the Ladies of Derby marked the Golden Jubilee by presenting Queen Victoria with a magnificent pair of Derby Crown vases designed by Richard Lunn and a plaque painted with a portrait of the Queen and ornamented with eight national emblems, eleven orders worn by the Queen and four panels containing heads representing painting, sculpture, poetry and music. In 1890 Queen Victoria granted the Derby Crown Company the use of the Royal Arms and the title 'Royal'. The company was renamed The Royal Crown Derby Porcelain Company.

The year 1890 was also important for the arrival of Désiré Leroy, the most distinguished artist/designer in the history of the company. Born in Les Loges, France, he began his career at the age of eleven as an apprentice at Sèvres. In 1874 he travelled to England to take up an appointment with Minton, where he executed a number of important services, including work for Queen Victoria. His arrival at Royal Crown Derby was to herald a new era in design and artistic standards. His training at Sèvres strongly influenced his work at Derby and the Sèvres style, already adopted during the Bloor period, gradually gained prominence over the Indo-Persian style which had dominated production for so many years.

Leroy's remarkable talents were utilised on some of the most intricate and beautiful shapes ever produced at Osmaston Road. Exquisite reserves of musical and scientific trophies, birds, butterflies and flowers were set within frames of richly raised gold on glorious ground colours. His flawless groundlaying and sense of colour were used in daring combinations, and his delicate 'jewelling', usually worked in white and turquoise, almost invariably embellished his Sèvres-style work. Leroy died in 1908 but the high standards he set continued to inspire artists of the calibre of Albert Gregory and Cuthbert Gresley.

Royal Crown Derby. 'Gadroon' dessert plate. Later replica of a service designed and executed by Leroy for presentation to Princess Mary of Teck and the Duke of York (later George V) on the occasion of their marriage in 1893. This example is painted by George Darlington. (Royal Crown Derby Museum)

Above: *Royal Crown Derby. Three of a set of six eggshell dessert plates, 'Royal' shape. Each has a different floral centre painted by Albert Gregory. Date: 1898. (Ronald William Raven Room)*

Above: *Royal Crown Derby. Superb pair of trophy pedestal vases, shape 1459, pattern F508. The painting of musical trophies is by Désiré Leroy. Date: 1906. (Royal Crown Derby Museum)*

Below: *Royal Crown Derby. Sèvres-style bon-bon dish with pierced borders. The floral centre is painted by Albert Gregory. Date: 1912. (Royal Crown Derby Museum)*

Above: *Royal Crown Derby. Gadroon-shaped dessert plate. The floral centre is painted by Albert Gregory. Date: 1904. (Ronald William Raven Room)*

Famous for the 'Gregory Rose', which is usually the focal point of his bouquets, Albert Gregory was probably the finest natural flower painter to have worked at the factory. Cuthbert Gresley was the only member of a family of distinguished watercolourists to choose ceramics as a vehicle for his art. He excelled in painting flowers and landscapes, which are noted for their fine detail and quality of 'distance'. In contrast, W. E. J. Dean painted tranquil shipping scenes in blue and white on tableware, plaques and ungilded, embossed ornamental wares known

Royal Crown Derby. Gadroon-shaped plate from a service presented to Sir Henry Howe Bemrose by the Unionists of Derby. Date: 1902. (Ronald William Raven Room)

Royal Crown Derby. Small plaque painted with a blue and white shipping scene by F. A. Marple. Date: 1903. (Royal Crown Derby Museum)

Royal Crown Derby. Oval plaque painted with a pastel shipping scene by W. E. J. Dean. Date: unmarked. (Barratt Bequest, Royal Crown Derby Museum)

as 'Derby Delft', although he often worked in full colour with elaborate gilt borders. He was also a fine landscape artist, and his love of the Derbyshire countryside in autumn is reflected in the autumnal palette he used. C. Remnant and F. A. Marple (a very fine flower painter) also painted blue and white shipping scenes.

Whilst printing accounted for a large volume of production, hand painting and gilding were still used on the majority of wares, including the famed Imari patterns that have been so much a feature of Derby production for more than two hundred years. The first recorded pattern

Royal Crown Derby. Sèvres-style dessert plate, pattern F518. Superbly painted with a rose, fruit and nut by Désiré Leroy. Royal Warrant mark. Date: 1906.

in the Osmaston Road Pattern Book Number 1 is Imari and most people associate Derby porcelain with the blue, red and gold of the Japanese-inspired Imari decoration. Of the three thousand Imari patterns produced at Derby since 1770, the most popular and extensively used patterns are: 198, an unnamed pattern of birds and chrysanthemums; 383, 'Old Crown Derby', a variation of pattern number 1, later renamed 'King's'; 6299, 'Derby Witches'; 1128, 'Old Imari'; and the extensively copied 2451, 'Traditional Imari'. While patterns 198, 383 and 6299 have been phased out over the years, 1128 and 2451 remain as popular today as they were when they were introduced in the 1880s. The skills of the designers in restructuring the complex elements of 1128 have enabled this famous pattern to be used on every conceivable shape, from elegant services to paperweights.

The 'Toy' shapes, introduced in 1904, were made entirely for ornament and not, as many believe, as travellers' samples. Measuring less than 3 inches (7 cm), and modelled in the form of domestic items such as teapots, kettles, saucepans and flat irons, these delightful pieces were mainly decorated with Imari patterns 198, 1128, 2451 and 6299, but

Left: *Royal Crown Derby. Sèvres-style large vase and cover, shape 1251, pattern F457. Superbly painted with musical instruments and flowers by Désiré Leroy. Date: 1899.*

Below: *Pages from Osmaston Road Pattern Book number 15, showing original watercolours for patterns 6297, 6299 and 6300. (Royal Crown Derby Museum)*

Left: *Royal Crown Derby. Group of 1128, 'Old Imari', giftware. The pattern was originally recorded in Pattern Book number 2, commenced 1882. Still in production. (Royal Crown Derby Museum)*

Below: *Royal Crown Derby. Tableware. Pattern 2451, 'Traditional Imari', pictured against the original artwork in Osmaston Road Pattern Book number 6, commenced 1887. The pattern is still in production. (Royal Crown Derby Museum)*

semi-Imari, standard tableware patterns and marine scenes were also used. What makes these tiny pieces so desirable and expensive is the fact that the decoration is a perfect miniaturisation of the whole pattern, with not a stroke missed. Production had largely ceased by 1940, but a new range of miniatures was introduced in 1996.

The art of flower making has been practised at Derby since the eighteenth century. Used to adorn birds, figurines and ornamental wares, each wafer-thin petal, stamen and sepal is individually modelled and assembled. Flower jewellery for brooches, earrings and stickpins was introduced shortly after the Second World War.

During the first quarter of the twentieth century some very fine and elaborate services were commissioned by Tiffany of New York on behalf of private clients. Probably the most celebrated of these was the

Royal Crown Derby. Group of Imari-decorated 'Toy' shapes: (clockwise from top left) coal scuttle, pattern 6299, 'Derby Witches'; witches' cauldron, pattern 6299; milk churn and bowl decorated with pattern 2649, an unnamed pattern sometimes referred to as 'The Barbed Wire' pattern because of the stiff little bows in the design. Dates: 1909, 1911, 1908. (Royal Crown Derby Museum)

33

Above: *Royal Crown Derby. Tableware from the celebrated service commissioned by Tiffany of New York on behalf of Judge Elbert H. Gary, who was a corporate lawyer. He formed the United States Steel Corporation in 1901 and founded the steel mill city of Gary, Indiana, in 1906. Date: 1909. (Royal Crown Derby Museum)*

extraordinary service produced in 1909 for the wealthy Judge Elbert H. Gary. It was unusual not only for the exceptionally large number of pieces and divisions of the service, but also for the meticulous attention to detail. The lavish raised gilding was executed by George Darlington, who succeeded Leroy as principal gilder and flower painter; the floral reserves and cartouches were by Gregory, and the fish and game centres were painted by Gresley and Charles Harris. In 1911 a service was commissioned for James Deering, an important American businessman, which was so elaborate that it took a team of the finest gilders eighteen months to complete the 120 pieces.

When the SS *Titanic* sailed from Southampton in 1912, she was carrying a large quantity of Royal Crown Derby, some of which was a consignment for Tiffany, but the rest was the tableware specially commissioned by Stoniers of Liverpool for use on board in the first-class restaurant. The company also made the china used on her sister ships, *Olympic* and *Britannic*. It also produced in 1912 a number of services painted by Gresley for use on the eleventh Duke of Bedford's yachts.

In the 1920s and 1930s figure production greatly increased: figures from the Derby Crown period were reintroduced and new figures were modelled by Mary Locke and Tom Wilkinson. Literary themes such as 'Robin Hood and Maid Marion', 'Don Quixote and Sancho Panza', 'Peter Pan' and 'Dr Syntax' became firm favourites.

In 1929 H. T. Robinson purchased a significant number of shares in Royal Crown Derby, thereby ending the Litherland–McInnes administration of the company. The Robinson family remained in control until 1963, with 'H.T.' as chairman until his death in 1953, when he was succeeded by

Royal Crown Derby. Plate from the service commissioned by Stoniers of Liverpool for use in the first-class restaurant on board the 'Titanic'. (Mr and Mrs Horsely)

his son. In 1935 the company acquired the King Street factory.

During the difficult years of the Second World War levels of production were maintained but, by order of the Board of Trade, severe restrictions were imposed on the amount of decorated china which could be made for the home market. Production was restricted to undecorated 'utility' tablewares, usually the 'Surrey' shape. Wares from this period are characterised by an ultra-thin body, a green backstamp and no year code. The immediate post-war years were also hard, with a shortage of raw materials, difficulties in recruiting staff and a desperate need to improve and modernise to meet the new Health and Safety regulations.

It was at this time that Arnold Mikelson, a gold medal sculptor from Latvia, joined the company and was responsible for modelling about sixty animal and bird studies. Modelled and hand-painted as close to nature as possible, his birds were to remain in production for more than fifty years.

To mark the coronation of Queen Elizabeth II in 1953, several manufacturers, including Derby, Royal Doulton, Minton, Worcester and Spode, combined skills to produce 'The Queen's Vase' to present to the Queen and the Commonwealth heads of state. Derby's contribution was a pair of platinum-coated heraldic beasts. In 1957 the citizens of Derby presented, for the Queen's personal use, a 120-piece service of 'Royal Pinxton Roses'. In 1958 a 'Mikado' bowl was presented to Cassidy's of Canada to mark the ten millionth piece of the pattern imported by them between 1950 and 1958.

Having survived the difficult post-war years, the company's affairs improved dramatically in the 1950s and 1960s when orders for lavishly decorated, expensive services were received from the oil-rich states of the Middle East. Typical of these was a service made for the Ruler of Qatar which contained three thousand pieces, including twelve dishes large enough to hold whole roast sheep. Other important overseas commissions included banqueting services for the Royal York Hotel, Toronto, and for the Governor General of Pakistan (for which the company received the Official Warrant), six hundred pieces for King Saud of Saudi Arabia, fifteen hundred pieces for the official use of the Prime Minister of Ceylon and a two-hundred-piece service for the Shah of Persia.

Royal Crown Derby. Garniture of 'Chelsea Birds', modelled by Arnold Mikelson. (Royal Crown Derby Museum)

John McLaughlin painting a 'Talbot'-shaped dessert dish from a botanical service designed by June Branscombe. (Royal Crown Derby Museum)

In 1964 Royal Crown Derby became a member of Allied English Potteries, a subsidiary of the Pearson Group, and in 1972 part of the Royal Doulton Group. This new influx of capital enabled the first-floor showroom to be converted into the elegant Royal Crown Derby Museum, which charts the company's development from 1750. In 1987 the Ronald William Raven Room, annexed to the museum, was opened to house a private collection of 135 pieces by many of Derby's most celebrated artists from 1750 to 1921.

In 1965 the company was asked to produce a service of forty-eight soup plates and matching dinner plates to be copied from a plate in Queen Elizabeth the Queen Mother's possession which had survived from a Derby service made in the late eighteenth century for the then Prince of Wales. During a visit to the factory in 1971, the Queen Mother was presented with a matching bowl, after which she honoured the company by commissioning a new shape, aptly named 'Queen's Gadroon'. Modelled and designed by June and Brian Branscombe, the first six designs on the new shape were launched in 1972 at Kedleston Hall, Derbyshire.

Despite the general trade recession of the 1970s production expanded. The 'Connoisseur Collection', which included a set of six yellow-ground coffee cans and stands painted with waterfowl and chicks by John McLaughlin, and a series of cabinet plates, painted with Derbyshire views by Michael Crawley, was produced. The other member of the artistic team was the highly gifted Stefan Nowacki, who later left to set up his own factory. A dinner and coffee service comprising 134 pieces of 'Derby Green Panel' was presented to Princess Anne and Captain Mark Phillips in 1973 on the occasion of their marriage.

In the 1980s an extended range of giftware was introduced and the first six Royal Crown Derby paperweights were launched in 1981 at Kedleston Hall. Modelled by Robert Jefferson, the Imari-decorated weights were originally intended purely as functional objects, although they have become

Royal Crown Derby. Yellow-ground coffee can and stand from the 'Connoisseur Collection', produced in a limited edition of fifty sets, each comprising six cans and stands hand-painted with British birds and their chicks in their natural habitat by John McLaughlin. 'Queen's Gadroon' shape. Date: 1972. (Royal Crown Derby Museum)

Right: *Royal Crown Derby. Paperweights: 'Penguin and Chick', 'Little Owl', 'Imari Polar Bear' and 'Ladybird'; still in production. (Royal Crown Derby Museum)*

highly collectable, with thousands of dedicated collectors across the world. In the early 1990s John Ablitt became responsible for the design of the paperweights. Since then the simple shapes and classic blue, red and gold of the early weights have been replaced by many new and brilliant colours and highly defined profiles. A range of 150 birds and animals, including exclusive limited editions commissioned by leading retailers and special promotional pieces, has resulted in a thriving second-hand market, with collectors prepared to pay high prices for discontinued models.

In 1990 the company celebrated the centenary of the granting of the title 'Royal' with two important exhibitions: 'Painters and the Derby China Works' (1748–1848), which incorporated watercolours from the *Bemrose Volumes*, presented to the museum in 1985, with matching porcelain, and '100 Royal Years', which included a celebration of the life and work of Désiré Leroy. It also produced a large covered urn and a crown paperweight, and a five-petal tray

Right: *Royal Crown Derby. Dressing-table set. The 'Honeysuckle' pattern was designed by Sue Rowe, Senior Designer. Date: 1991. (Royal Crown Derby Museum)*

Left: *Royal Crown Derby. Christmas plate, the first in a series of six designed by Sue Rowe. Date: 1991. (Royal Crown Derby Museum)*

1880	1881	1882	1883	1884	1885	1886	1887	1888	1889	1890	1891

1892	1893	1894	1895	1896	1897	1898	1899	1900	1901	1902	1903

1904	1905	1906	1907	1908	1909	1910	1911	1912	1913	1914	1915

1916	1917	1918	1919	1920	1921	1922	1923	1924	1925	1926	1927

1928	1929	1930	1931	1932	1933	1934	1935	1936	1937	1938	1939
										I	II

1940	1941	1942	1943	1944	1945	1946	1947	1948	1949	1950	1951
III	IV	V	VI	VII	VIII	IX	X	XI	XII	XIII	XIV

Royal Crown Derby date marks. From 1938 the marks follow on as Roman numerals, beginning with I in 1938 and reaching LXII in 1999. In 2000 a special mark was used, comprising two interlaced Ms, with the normal sequence of Roman numerals resuming with LXIV in 2001. To avoid confusion, note the root year codes 'X' and 'V' denoting 1901 and 1904 are accompanied by 'England', while the Roman numerals 'V' and 'X' denoting 1942 and 1947 are accompanied by 'Made in England'.

The special year mark for 2000.

designed by June Branscombe was presented to every employee. In 1991 the first Christmas plate was launched; designed by Sue Rowe and issued in a limited edition of five hundred, the plate was the first of a themed series of six.

In response to the rapidly expanding range of paperweights and the increasing range of giftware, the Royal Crown Derby Collectors' Guild was launched in 1994. In 1998 the Royal Crown Derby Visitors' Centre was opened.

The closing years of the twentieth century were a period of great activity as Royal Crown Derby prepared for the exciting challenge of a double celebration: the Millennium and the 250th anniversary of the earliest dated piece of Derby porcelain. Twenty special productions and specially commissioned limited editions were produced, including the humorous Millennium Bug paperweight and the spectacular 8 foot (2.43 metre) Anniversary Fountain, designed by John Ablitt and inspired by the minarets of the East (see page 40).

Marks used at the Osmaston Road factory 1877 to the present

Derby Crown Period, usually in black; 1877–90.

Royal Crown Derby; 1890–1940. Between c.1930 and 1940 this mark appears in red, grey, pink and pale green, sometimes without a year code.

Royal Crown Derby wartime mark in dark green; 1940–5. Usually without year code. Also used on undecorated utility wares.

Royal Crown Derby; 1964–75.

Royal Crown Derby; 1976 to the present.

Further reading

Barrett, Franklin A., and Thorpe, Arthur L. *Derby Porcelain*. Faber & Faber, 1971.

Battie, David. *Sotheby's Concise Encyclopaedia of Porcelain*. Conran Octopus, 1990.

Bemrose, William. *Bow, Chelsea and Derby China*. Bemrose & Sons, 1898.

Bradley, Peter. *Derby Porcelain 1750–1798*. Thomas Heaneage, 1990.

Bradshaw, Peter. *Derby Porcelain Figures 1750–1848*. Faber & Faber, 1990.

Gilhespy, F. Brayshaw. *Derby Porcelain*. McGibbon & Kee, 1961.

Gilhespy, F. Brayshaw, and Budd, Dorothy M. *Royal Crown Derby*. Charles Skilton, 1964.

Challand, Myra. *Derby China through Three Centuries*. J. Hall & Sons, 1991.

Cox, Ian. *Royal Crown Derby Paperweights: A Collector's Guide*. Merrell Holberton, 1997.

Cox, Ian. *Royal Crown Derby Imari Wares*. Merrell Holberton, 1999.

Gibson, Hugh. *A Case of Fine China 1875–1890*. Royal Crown Derby, 1993.

Hoyte, Anthony. *The Charles Norman Collection of Eighteenth Century Derby Porcelain*. Nuffield Press, 1996.

Twitchett, John. *Derby Porcelain*. Barrie & Jenkins, 1980.

Twitchett, John, and Murdoch, John. *Painters and the Derby China Works*. Trefoil, 1987.

Twitchett, John, and Sandon, Henry. *Landscapes on Derby and Worcester Porcelain*. Henderson & Stirk, 1984.

Twitchett, John, and Bailey, Betty. *Royal Crown Derby*. Antique Collectors' Club, third edition 1988. (First published by Barrie & Jenkins, 1976.)

Not Just a Bed of Roses. Usher Gallery, 1996.

Places to visit

UNITED KINGDOM

Birmingham Museum and Art Gallery, Chamberlain Square, Birmingham B3 3DH. Telephone: 0121 303 2834. Website: www.bmag.org.uk

The British Museum, Great Russell Street, London WC1B 3DG. Telephone: 020 7323 8000 or 020 7323 8299. Website: www.british-museum.ac.uk

Chatsworth House, Chatsworth, Bakewell, Derbyshire DE45 1PP. Telephone: 01246 565300. Website: www.chatsworth-house.co.uk

Derby Museum and Art Gallery, The Strand, Derby DE1 1BS. Telephone: 01332 716654. Website: www.derby.gov.uk/museums

Harewood House, Harewood, Leeds LS17 9LQ. Telephone: 0113 218 1010. Website: www.harewood.org

Kedleston Hall, Kedleston, Derby DE22 5JH. Telephone: 01332 842191. Website: www.nationaltrust.org.uk

Royal Crown Derby Museum and Visitors Centre, 194 Osmaston Road, Derby DE23 8JZ. Telephone: 01332 712800. Website: www.royal-crown-derby.co.uk

Victoria and Albert Museum, Cromwell Road, South Kensington, London SW7 2RL. Telephone: 020 7942 2000. Website: www.vam.ac.uk

Wallace Collection, Hertford House, Manchester Square, London W1U 3BN. Telephone: 020 7563 9500. Website: www.wallacecollection.org

CANADA

George Gardiner Museum of Ceramic Art, 111 Queen's Park, Toronto, Ontario, Canada M5S 2C7. Telephone: 001 (0) 416 586 8080. Website: www.gardinermuseum.on.ca

Royal Ontario Museum, 100 Queen's Park, Toronto, Ontario, Canada M5S 2C6. Website: www.rom.on.ca

The Anniversary Fountain, designed by John Ablitt and manufactured under his direction. The concept involves a Brazilian mahogany base concealing a pump and supporting a mosaic-lined bowl from which rises a column which in turn supports a fringed gallery, topped by a cupola and crown. The crown is a replica of the massive cast-iron crown which sits on top of the dome on the roof of the Royal Crown Derby factory, in Osmaston Road, Derby.
The water is pumped from a tank concealed in the base, up the column into a hidden reservoir beneath the gallery, and then flows down strands of filament threaded with clear and coloured crystal. Light is projected from a hidden source in the base through fibre optic cables in the column, to illuminate the gallery and the waterfall.
The fountain is made up of 1500 individual tiles in fine bone china, decorated with ceramic enamels and hand-painted in pure 24 carat gold. The tiles are decorated with Imari patterns in traditional colours, and aquatic animals. The Hon. Hugh Gibson is admiring the fountain.